HAL•LEONARD

Classic Songs

Arranged by GARY MEISNER

Recorded by Jim Reith at BeatHouse Music, Milwaukee, WI
Accordion by Gary Meisner
Bass by George Welland
Drums by Steve Colvin

ISBN 978-1-4234-9559-8

HAL•LEONARD®
CORPORATION
7777 W. BLUEMOUND RD. P.O. BOX 13819 MILWAUKEE, WI 53213

In Australia Contact:
Hal Leonard Australia Pty. Ltd.
4 Lentara Court
Cheltenham, Victoria, 3192 Australia
Email: ausadmin@halleonard.com.au

For all works contained herein:
Unauthorized copying, arranging, adapting, recording, Internet posting, public performance,
or other distribution of the printed or recorded music in this publication is an infringement of copyright.
Infringers are liable under the law.

Visit Hal Leonard Online at
www.halleonard.com

CARNIVAL OF VENICE

By JULIUS BENEDICT

TRACKS
1–2

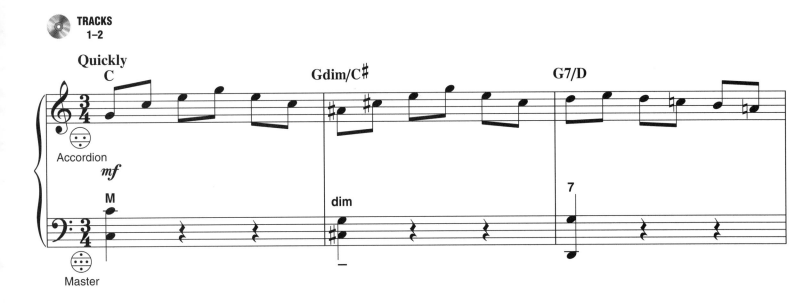

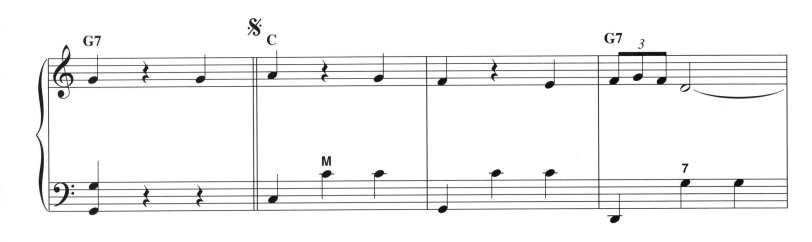

Copyright © 2010 by HAL LEONARD CORPORATION
International Copyright Secured   All Rights Reserved

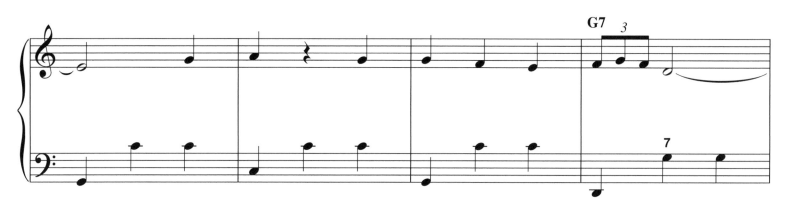

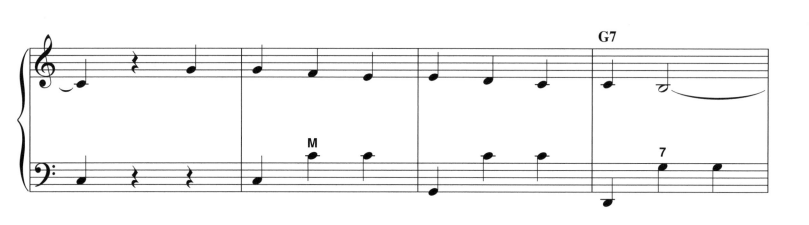

4

To Coda ⊕

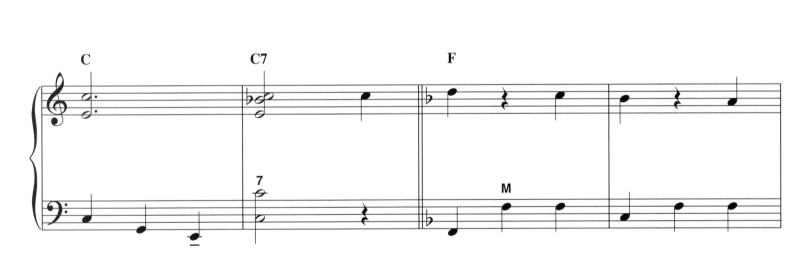

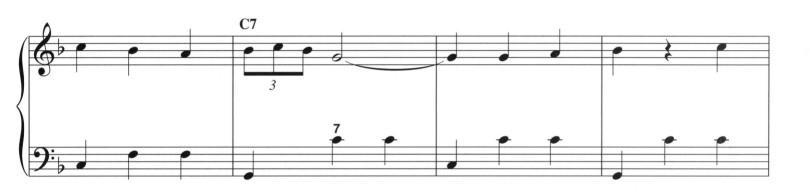

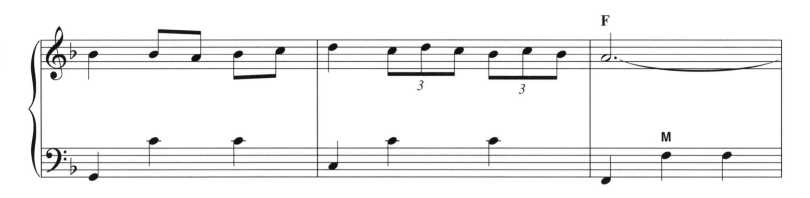

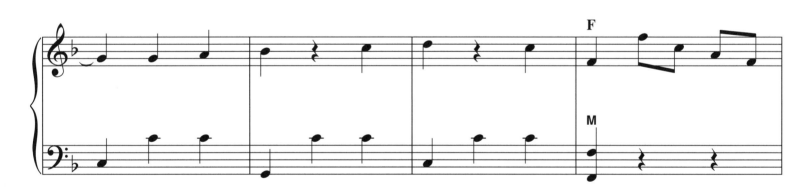

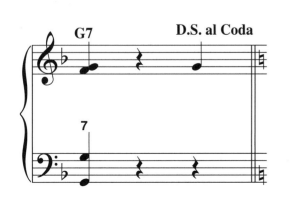

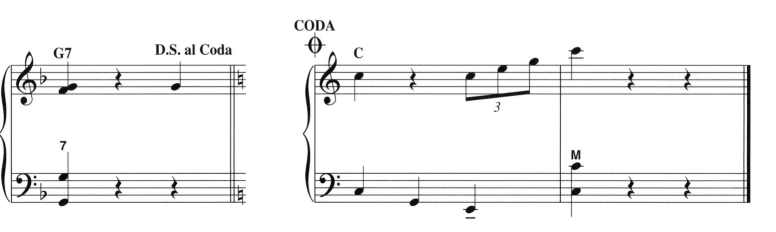

CIRIBIRIBIN

Words and Music by
ANTONIO PESTALOZZA

Copyright © 2010 by HAL LEONARD CORPORATION
International Copyright Secured   All Rights Reserved

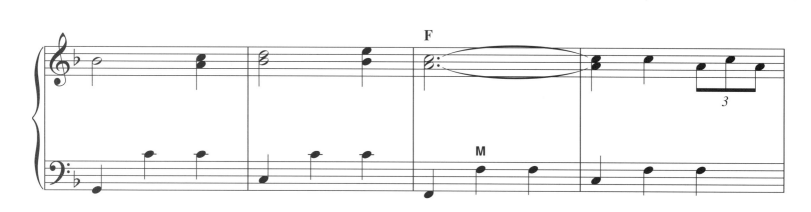

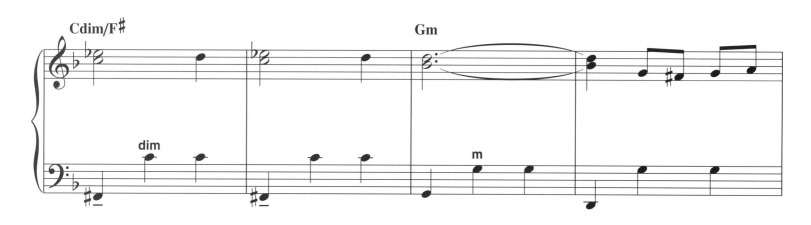

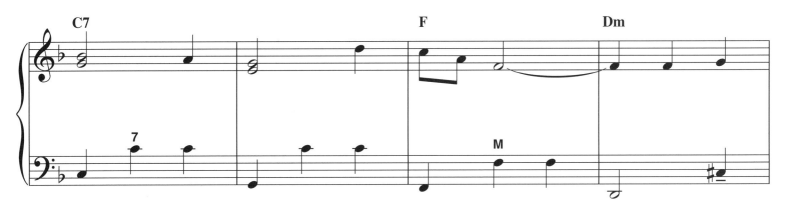

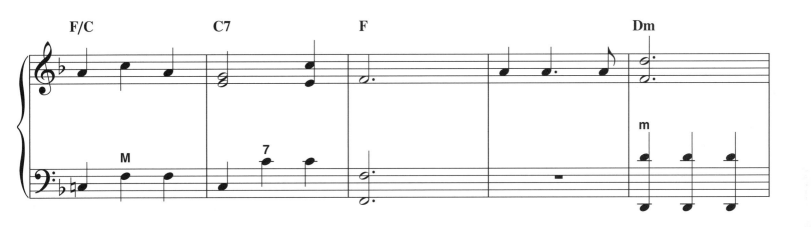

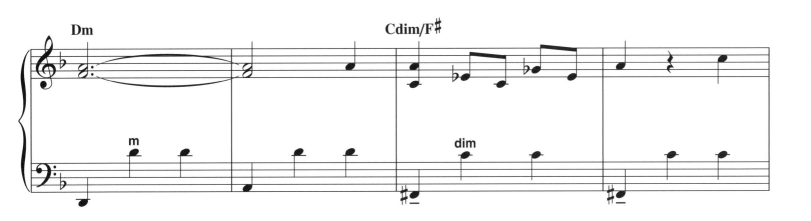

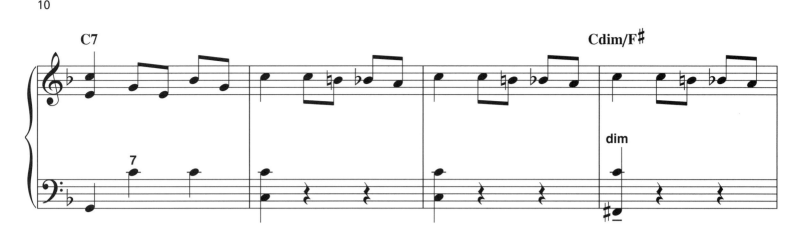

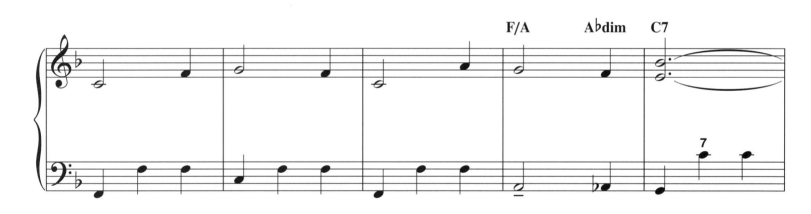

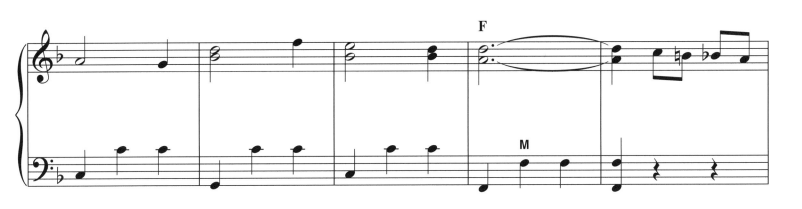

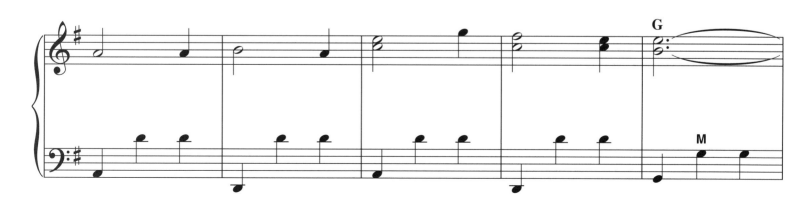

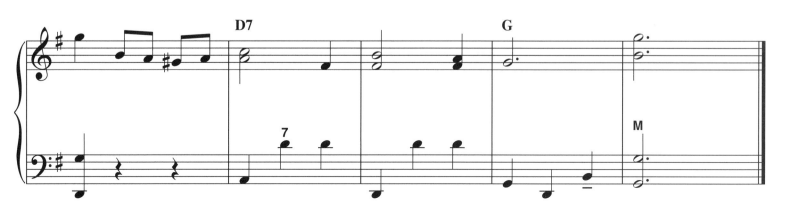

COME BACK TO SORRENTO

By ERNESTO DE CURTIS

Copyright © 2010 by HAL LEONARD CORPORATION
International Copyright Secured   All Rights Reserved

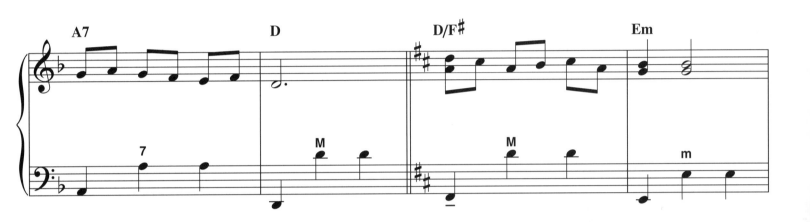

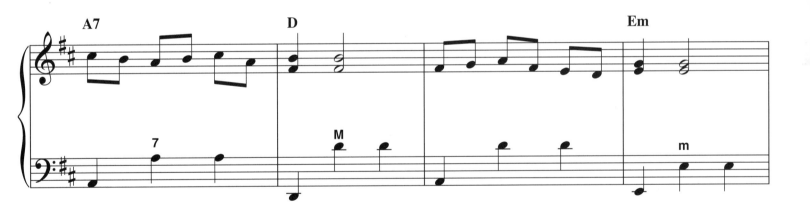

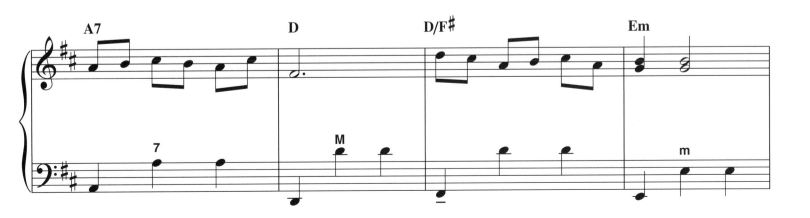

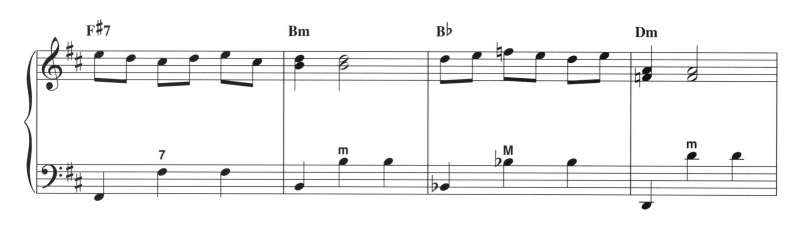

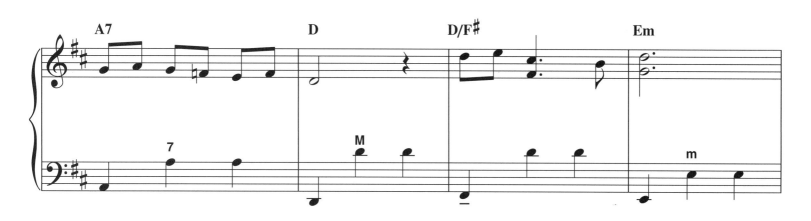

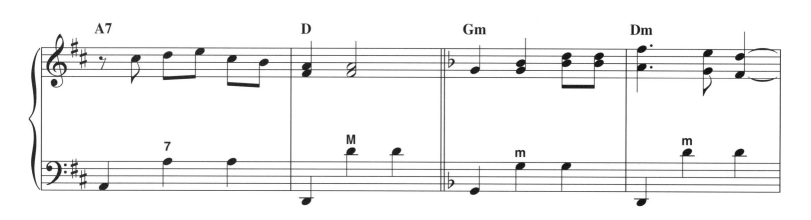

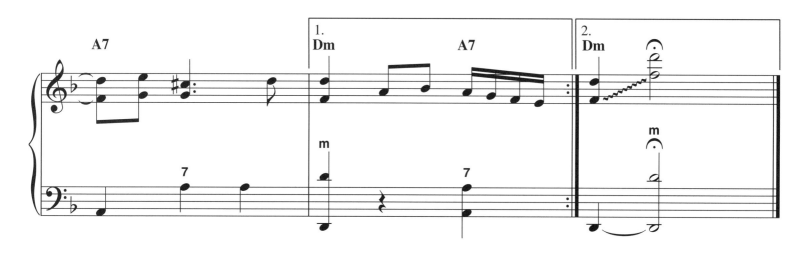

IN THE GOOD OLD SUMMERTIME

Words by REN SHIELDS
Music by GEORGE EVANS

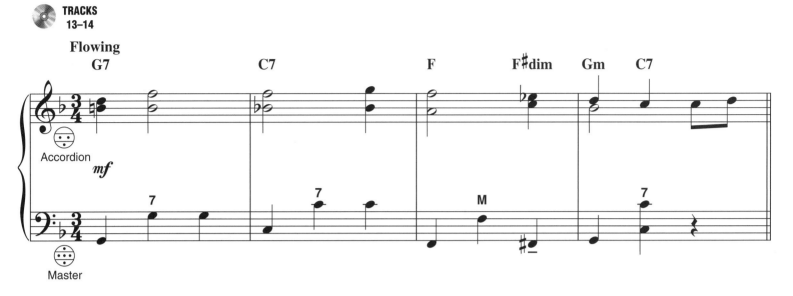

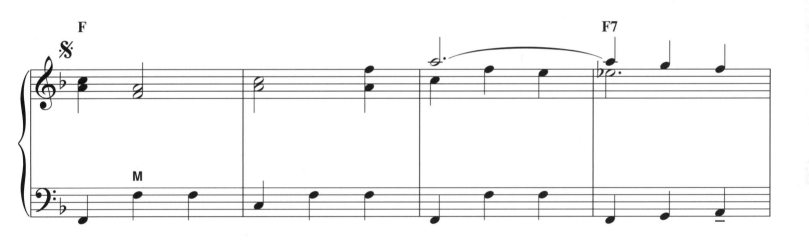

Copyright © 2010 by HAL LEONARD CORPORATION
International Copyright Secured   All Rights Reserved

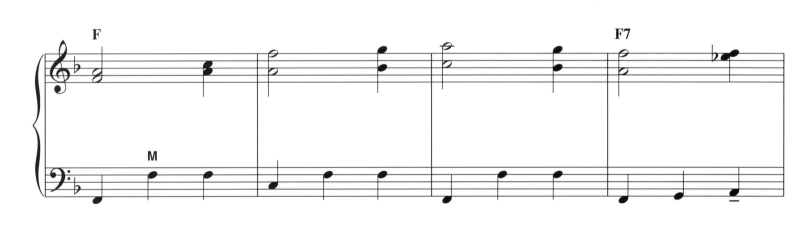

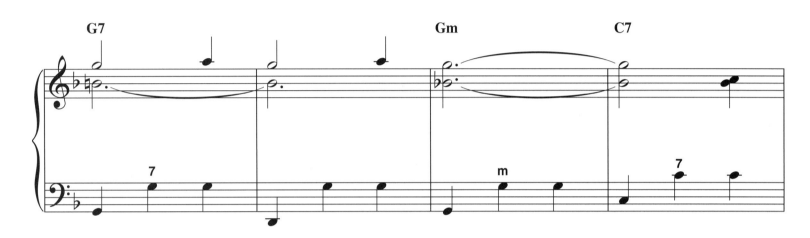

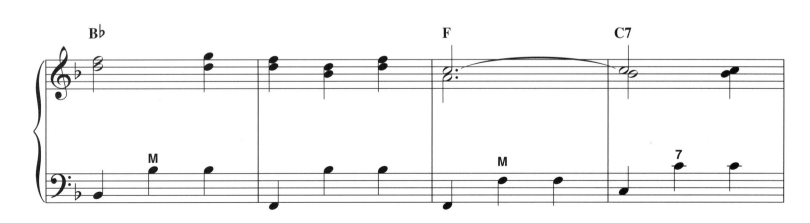

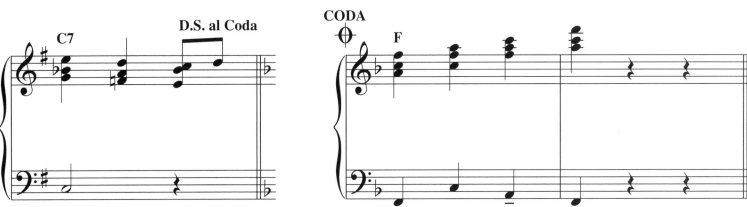

FASCINATION
(Valse Tzigane)

By F.D. MARCHETTI

TRACKS
7–8

Copyright © 2010 by HAL LEONARD CORPORATION
International Copyright Secured   All Rights Reserved

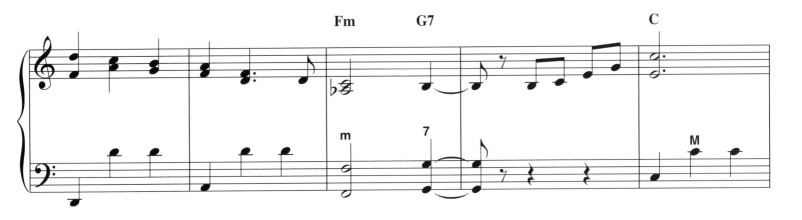

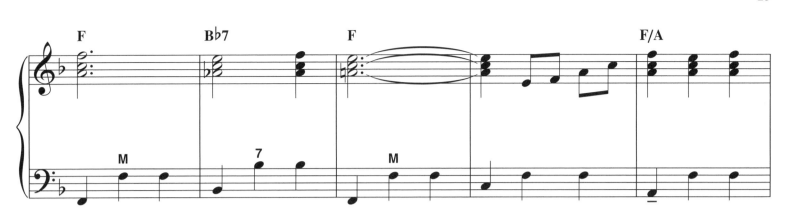

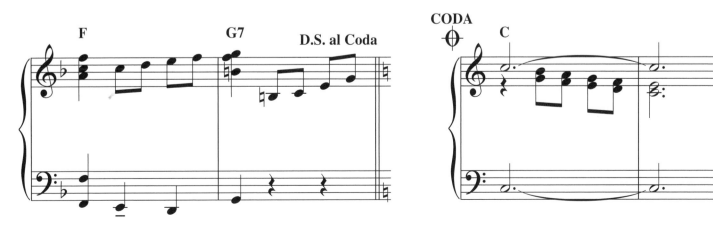

FUNICULI, FUNICULA

Words and Music by
LUIGI DENZA

TRACKS
9–10

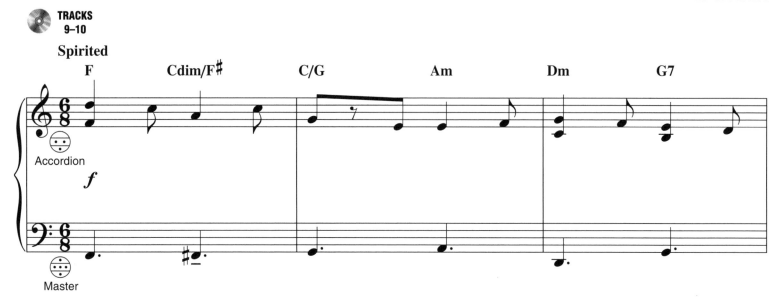

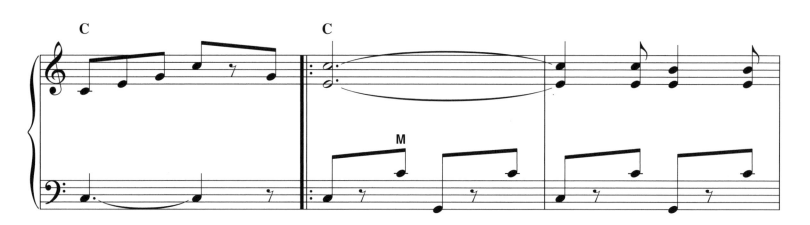

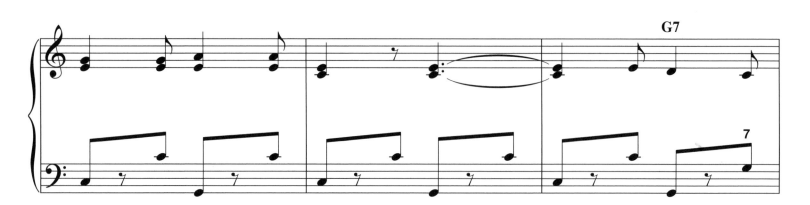

Copyright © 2010 by HAL LEONARD CORPORATION
International Copyright Secured   All Rights Reserved

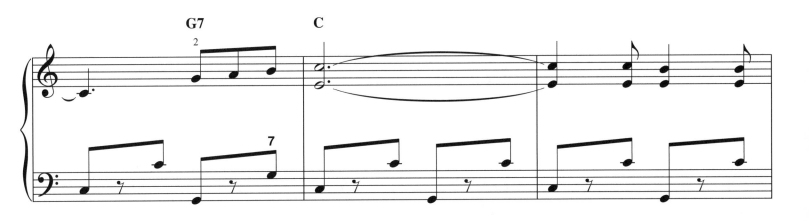

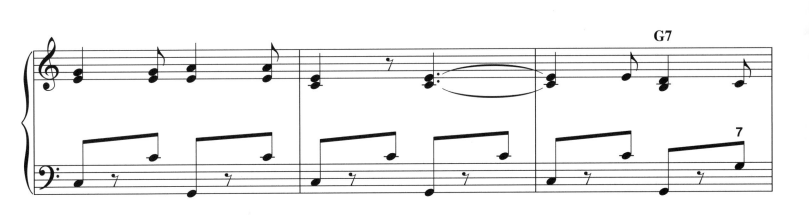

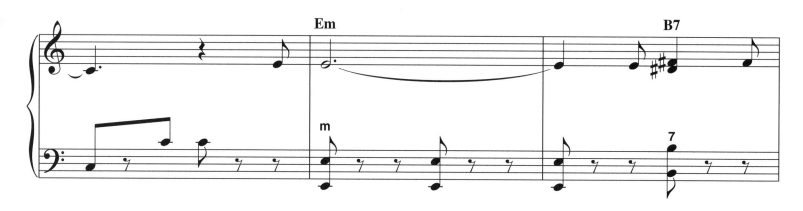

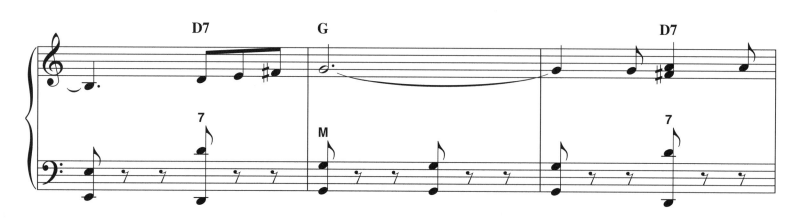

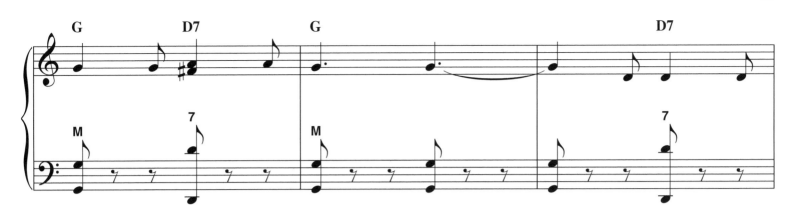

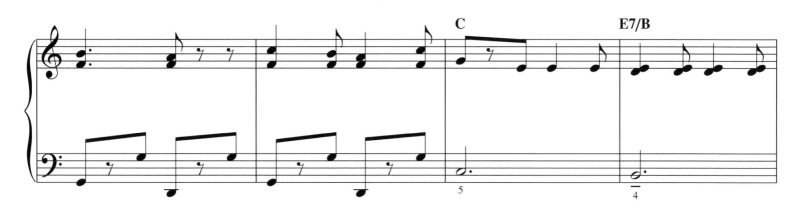

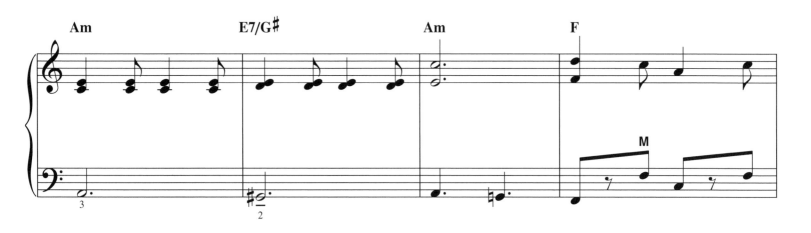

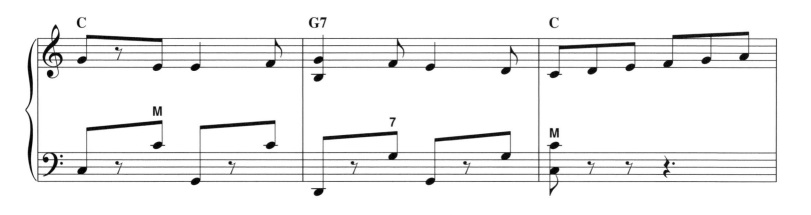

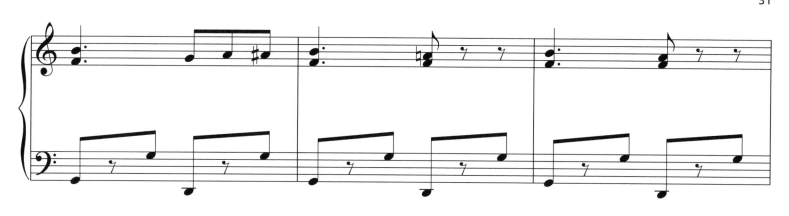

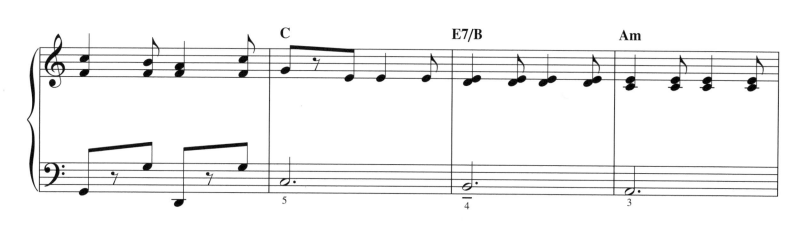

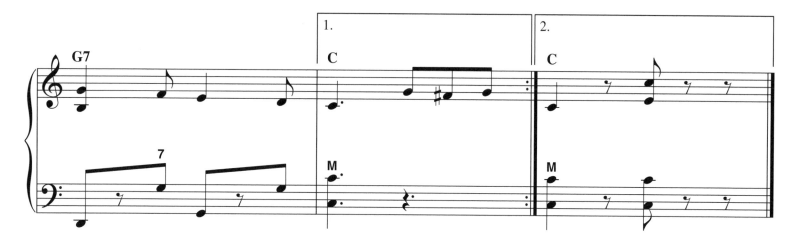

I LOVE YOU TRULY

Words and Music by
CARRIE JACOBS-BOND

TRACKS
11–12

Slowly, with expression

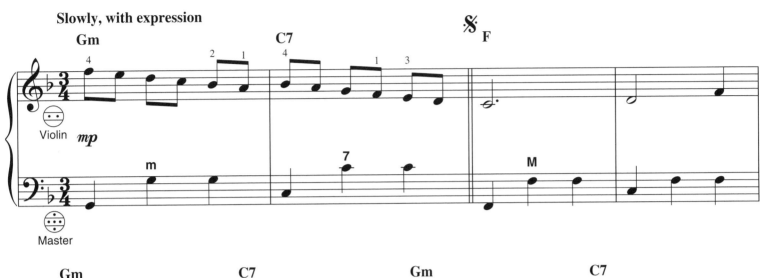

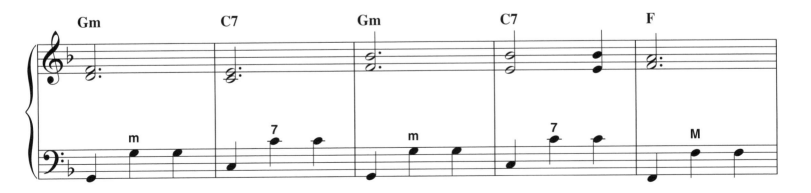

Copyright © 2010 by HAL LEONARD CORPORATION
International Copyright Secured   All Rights Reserved

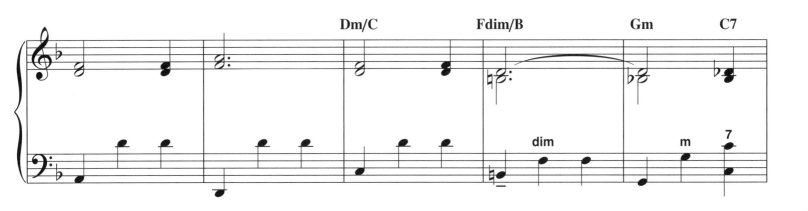

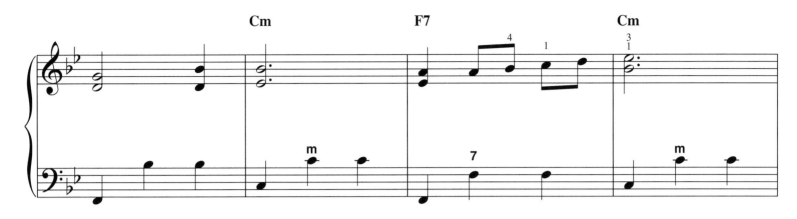

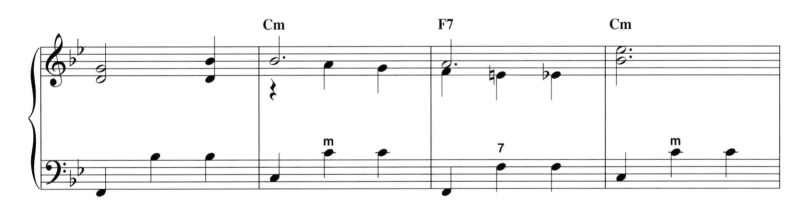

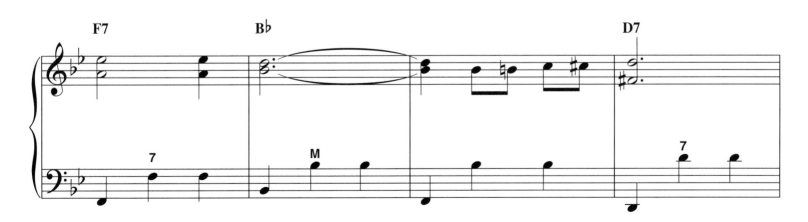

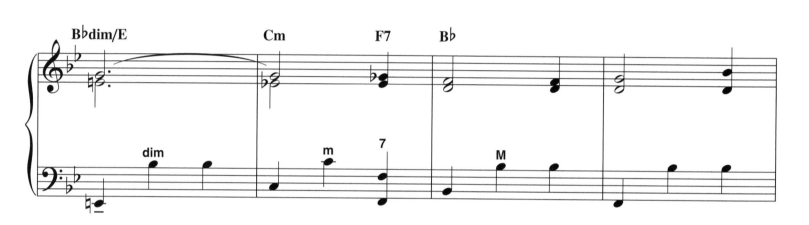

MELODY OF LOVE

By H. ENGELMANN

TRACKS
15–16

Copyright © 2010 by HAL LEONARD CORPORATION
International Copyright Secured   All Rights Reserved

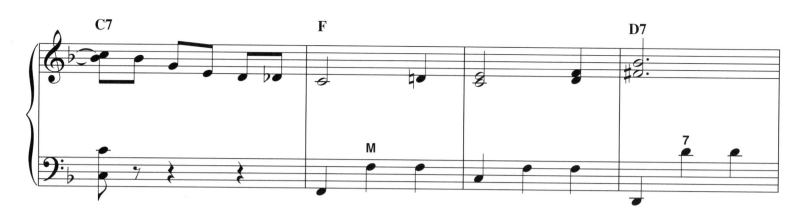

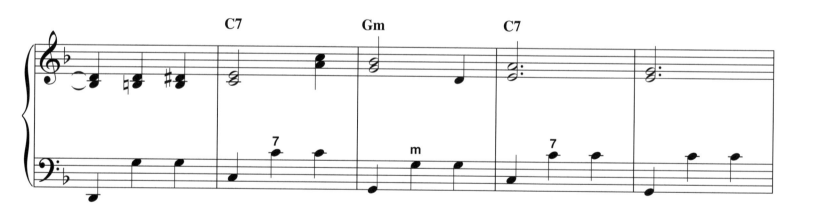

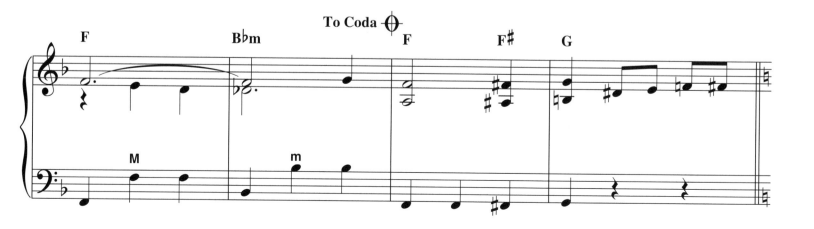

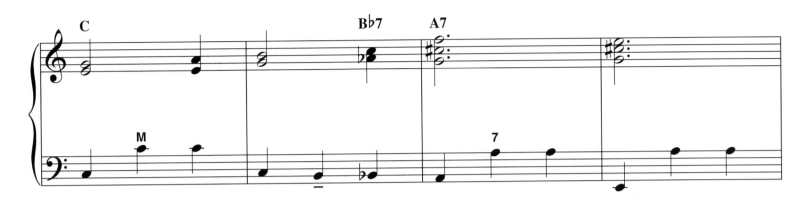

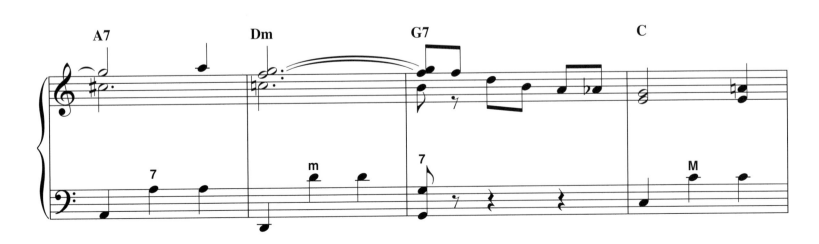

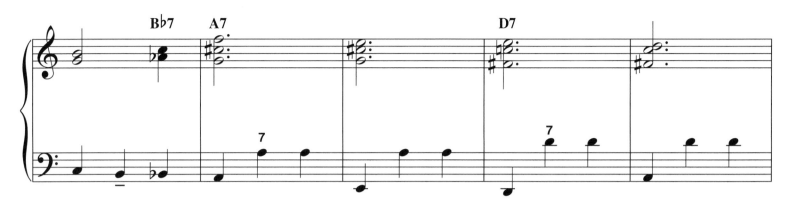

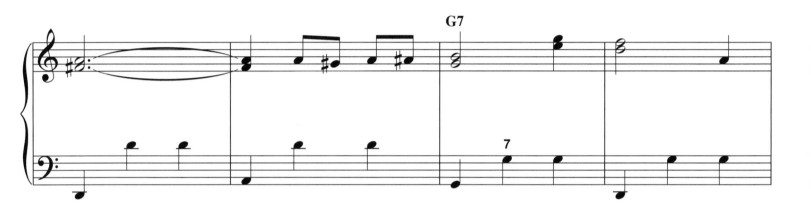

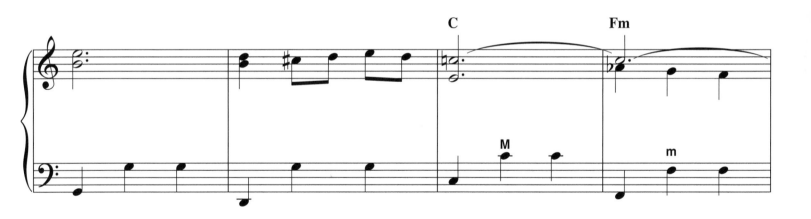

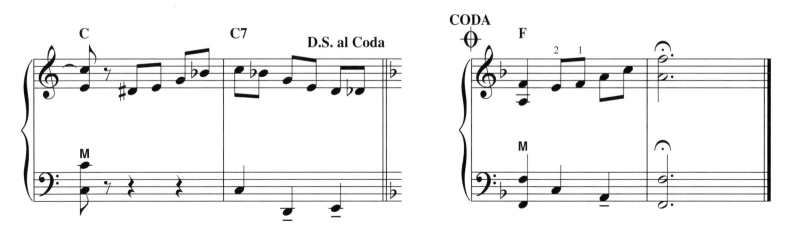

PEG O' MY HEART

Words by ALFRED BRYAN
Music by FRED FISHER

TRACKS
17–18

Copyright © 2010 by HAL LEONARD CORPORATION
International Copyright Secured   All Rights Reserved

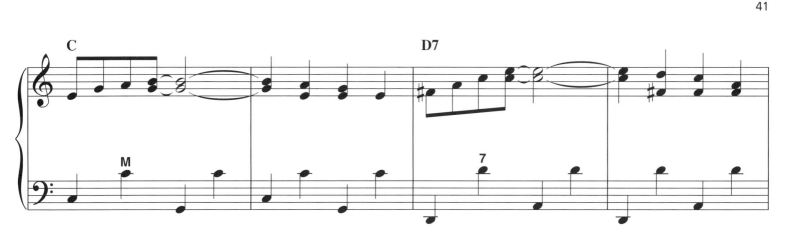

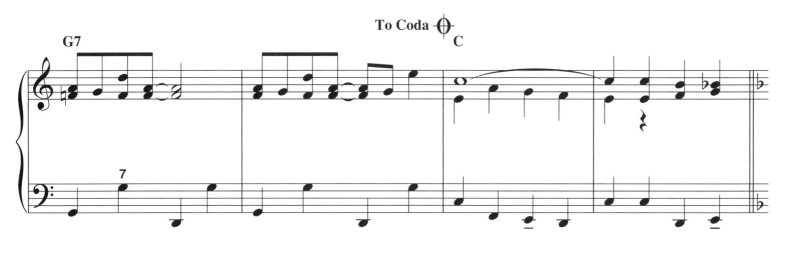

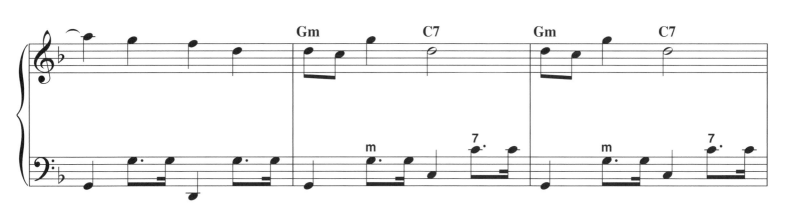

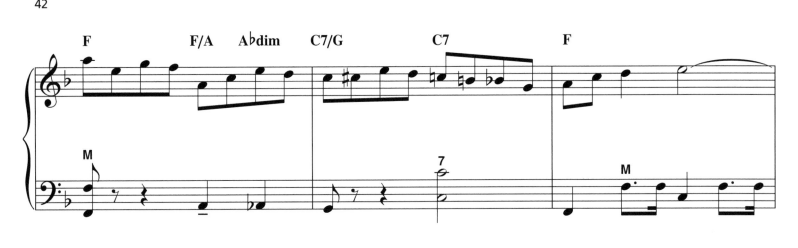

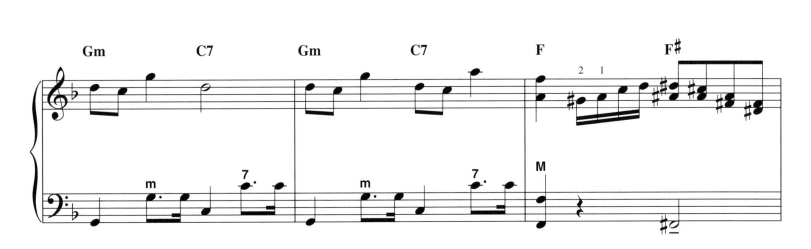

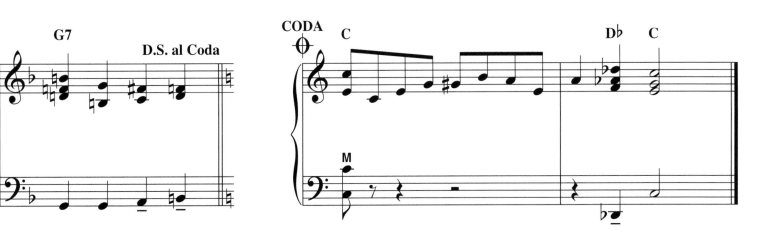

WHEN IRISH EYES ARE SMILING

Words by CHAUNCEY OLCOTT
and GEORGE GRAFF, JR.
Music by ERNEST R. BALL

TRACKS
19–20

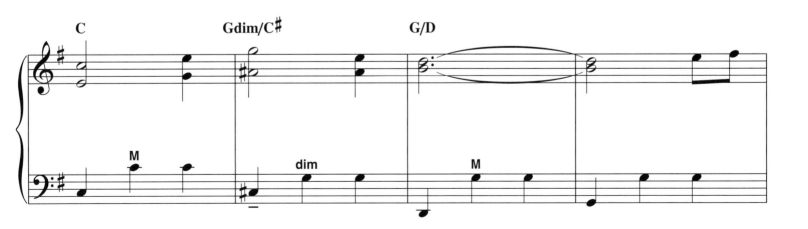

Copyright © 2010 by HAL LEONARD CORPORATION
International Copyright Secured   All Rights Reserved

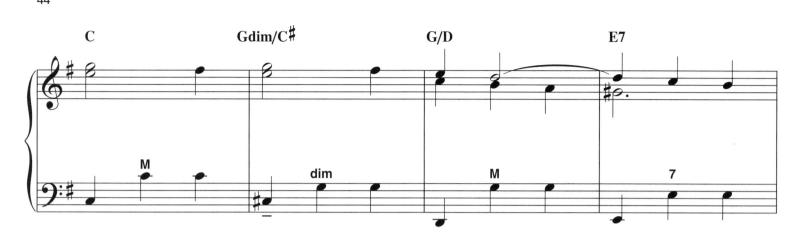

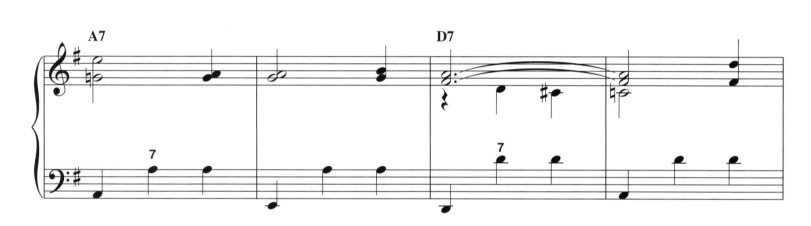

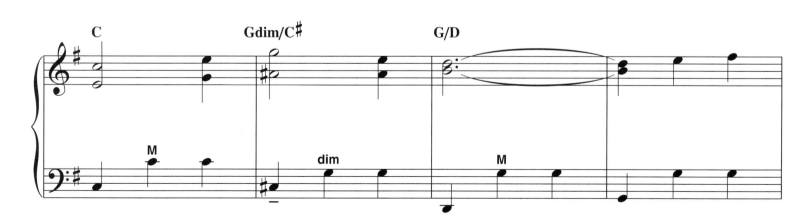

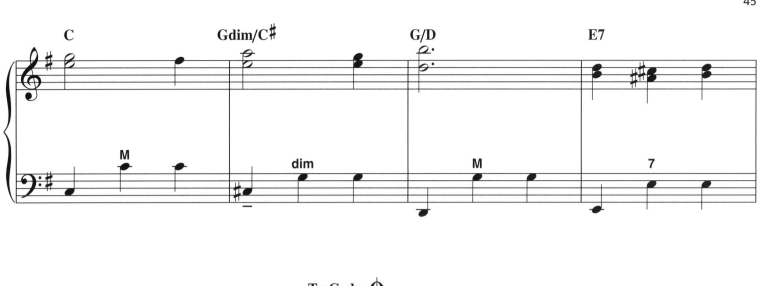

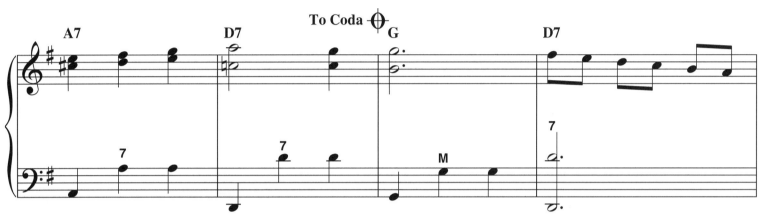

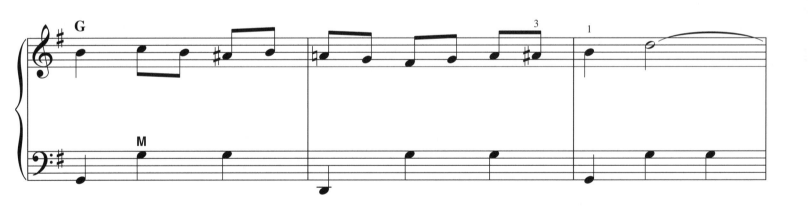

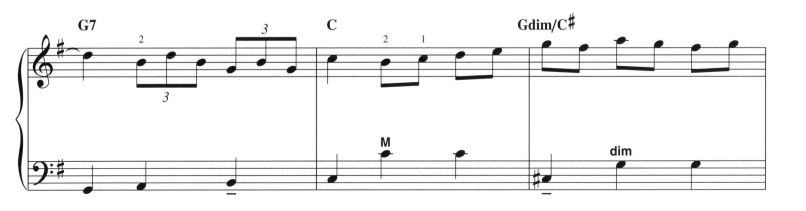

46

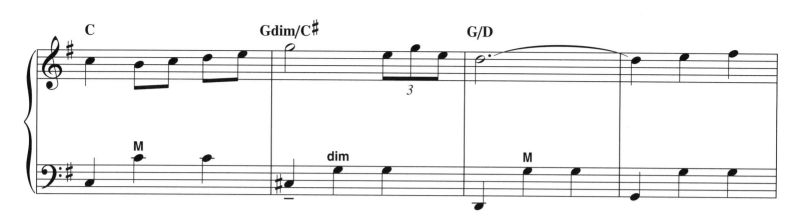

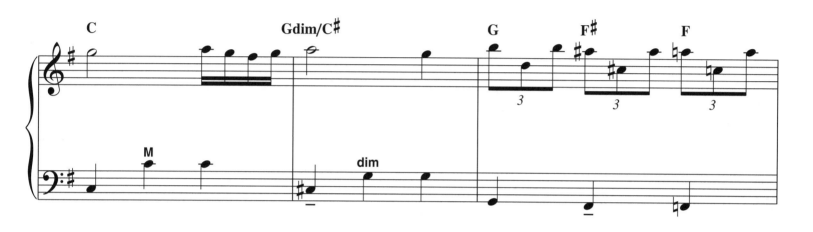

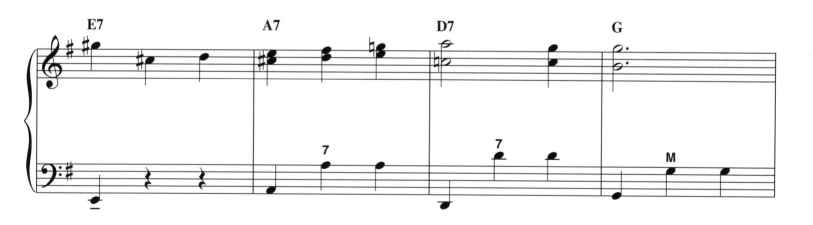

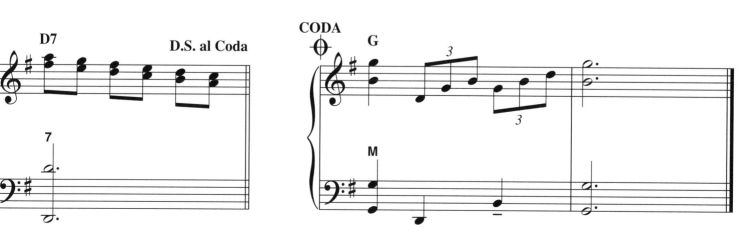

A COLLECTION OF ALL-TIME FAVORITES FOR ACCORDION

ACCORDION FAVORITES
arr. Gary Meisner

16 all-time favorites, arranged for accordion, including: Can't Smile Without You • Could I Have This Dance • Endless Love • Memory • Sunrise, Sunset • I.O.U. • and more.
00359012 ....$10.95

ALL-TIME FAVORITES FOR ACCORDION
arr. Gary Meisner

20 must-know standards arranged for accordions. Includes: Ain't Misbehavin' • Autumn Leaves • Crazy • Hello, Dolly! • Hey, Good Lookin' • Moon River • Speak Softly, Love • Unchained Melody • The Way We Were • Zip-A-Dee-Doo-Dah • and more.
00311088 ....$10.95

THE BEATLES GREATEST HITS FOR ACCORDION

15 of the Beatles greatest hits arranged for accordion. Includes: Lucy in the Sky with Diamonds • A Hard Day's Night • Yellow Submarine • All My Loving • Yesterday • Michelle • Hey Jude • more.
00359121 ....$12.99

BROADWAY FAVORITES
arr. Ken Kotwitz

A collection of 17 wonderful show songs, including: Don't Cry for Me Argentina • Getting to Know You • If I Were a Rich Man • Oklahoma • People Will Say We're in Love • We Kiss in a Shadow.
00490157 ....$9.95

CHRISTMAS SONGS FOR ACCORDION

17 holiday hits, including: The Chipmunk Song • Frosty the Snow Man • A Holly Jolly Christmas • Jingle-Bell Rock • Pretty Paper • Rudolph the Red-Nosed Reindeer.
00359477 ....$8.99

CONTEMPORARY HITS FOR ACCORDION
arr. Gary Meisner

15 songs, including: I Left My Heart in San Francisco • Just the Way You Are • Longer • September Morn • Somewhere Out There • Through the Years • and more.
00359491 ....$9.95

DISNEY MOVIE FAVORITES

Students will love playing these 12 songs from the Disney favorites *Aladdin, Beauty and the Beast,* and *The Little Mermaid.* Songs include: Under the Sea • Be Our Guest • A Whole New World • and more!
00311632 ....$9.95

ITALIAN SONGS FOR ACCORDION
arr. Gary Meisner

17 favorite Italian standards arranged for accordion, including: Carnival of Venice • Ciribiribin • Come Back to Sorrento • Funiculi, Funicula • La donna è mobile • La Spagnola • 'O Sole Mio • Santa Lucia • Tarantella • and more.
00311089 ....$9.95

LATIN FAVORITES FOR ACCORDION
arr. Gary Meisner

20 Latin favorites, including: Bésame Mucho (Kiss Me Much) • The Girl from Ipanema • How Insensitive (Insensatez) • Perfidia • Spanish Eyes • So Nice (Summer Samba) • and more.
00310932 ....$10.99

THE SONGS OF ANDREW LLOYD WEBBER FOR ACCORDION

10 of his best, including: All I Ask of You • Any Dream Will Do • As If We Never Said Goodbye • I Don't Know How to Love Him • Love Changes Everything • The Music of the Night • Old Deuteronomy • Think of Me • Unexpected Song • With One Look.
00310152 ....$10.95

POLKA FAVORITES
arr. Kenny Kotwitz

An exciting new collection of 16 songs, including: Beer Barrel Polka • Liechtensteiner Polka • My Melody of Love • Paloma Blanca • Pennsylvania Polka • Too Fat Polka • and more.
00311573 ....$10.95

WALTZ FAVORITES
arr. Kenny Kotwitz

Accordion arrangements of 17 classic waltzes, including: Alice Blue Gown • I Love You Truly • I Wonder Who's Kissing Her Now • I'll Be with You in Apple Blossom Time • Let Me Call You Sweetheart • Let the Rest of the World Go By • My Buddy • and more.
00310576 ....$9.95

LAWRENCE WELK'S POLKA FOLIO

More than 50 famous polkas, schottisches and waltzes arranged for piano and accordion, including: Blue Eyes • Budweiser Polka • Clarinet Polka • Cuckoo Polka • The Dove Polka • Draw One Polka • Gypsy Polka • Helena Polka • International Waltzes • Let's Have Another One • Schnitzelbank • Shuffle Schottische • Squeeze Box Polka • Waldteufel Waltzes • and more.
00123218 ....$10.95

Prices, contents & availability
subject to change without notice.

Disney artwork & characters © Disney Enterprises, Inc.

FOR MORE INFORMATION,
SEE YOUR LOCAL MUSIC DEALER,
OR WRITE TO:

HAL•LEONARD®
CORPORATION
7777 W. BLUEMOUND RD. P.O. BOX 13819
MILWAUKEE, WISCONSIN 53213

Visit Hal Leonard Online at **www.halleonard.com**